The Secret of
Loch Ness

T0327870

Written by Sarah Rice

Illustrated by Monica Auriemma

Collins

Have you heard the story of Loch Ness?

Thousands of people visit this Scottish loch every year to photograph it and catch a glimpse of its secret.

They are all searching for the Loch Ness Monster.

3

Loch Ness is a huge, deep lake in the Scottish Highlands.

Fact!
Loch is the Scottish word for lake.

The story of the Loch Ness Monster began over a thousand years ago. A man called Saint Columba claimed he saw an incredible creature in the loch.

Later, in the 1930s, some people said they saw a creature with a huge body, a wavy neck and skin like an elephant.

Fact!
The Loch Ness Monster
is also called Nessie.

In 1934, a man called Robert Wilson took a photograph. It showed the creature's head and neck emerging from the water.

11

Experts found that the photo was a hoax –
it was not a real monster.

It was really a plastic head on a toy boat.

The photograph was fake, but other people say they have spotted the monster in the loch.

What could it be?

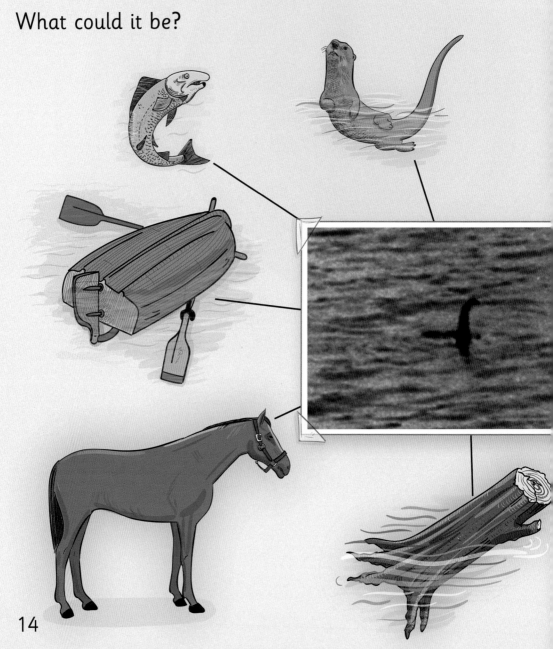

15

From the 1970s, people searched the loch.
They used sonar beams to take pictures of
objects under the water.

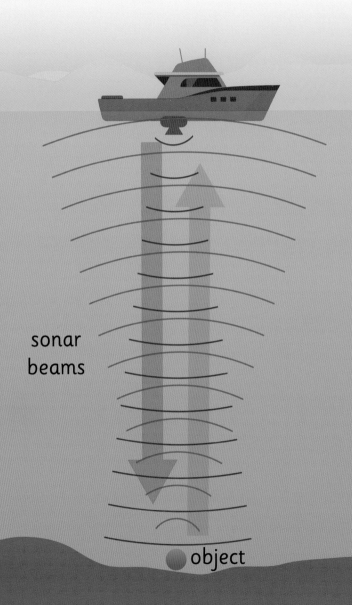

sonar
beams

object

In 1975, researchers saw a big object on screen, but they couldn't tell whether it was the monster.

In 2018, scientists from around the world tested water samples from Loch Ness. Their work helps us understand what lives in the loch.

Fact!
These scientists study underwater life.

No one has ever seen Nessie for sure.
However, people will always be interested
in the secret of Loch Ness!

Timeline

1000 years ago   1930s

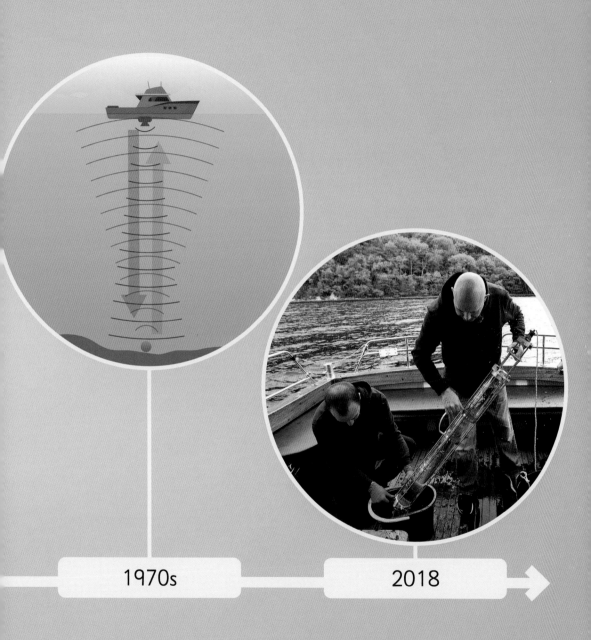

1970s

2018

🐾 Review: After reading 🐾

Use your assessment from hearing the children read to choose any GPCs, words or tricky words that need additional practice.

Read 1: Decoding

- Look at pages 2 and 6. Ask the children to find two words that have the sound /ch/ (*catch, creature*).
- Can the children point to the letters that make the /ch/ sound? (*tch, ture*)
- Make a list of some other /ch/ words and group them by their spelling. (e.g. *ch: searched; tch: match, watch; ture: adventure, capture*)

Read 2: Prosody

- Choose two double page spreads and model reading with expression to the children.
- Ask the children to have a go at reading the same pages with expression.
- Model reading a page of Loch Ness facts as if you are a nature documentary presenter. Use your voice to create interest. Ask the children to read a page in the same manner.

Read 3: Comprehension

- For every question ask the children how they know the answer. Ask:
  o What is the secret of Loch Ness? (*whether there is a monster in the loch*)
  o Where is Loch Ness? (*Scotland, the Scottish Highlands*)
  o Can you remember who first claimed to see the monster? (*Saint Columba*)
  o Do you think the Loch Ness Monster exists? Why?

Welcome to My Home!

Contents

Written by Catherine Baker

Collins

Welcome to our homes!

Hello! I'm Ana.

Ana, Brazil

Eric, Kenya

I'm Eric.

2

Come and see the places where we live!

Jodie, China

I'm Jodie!

3

Ana's home in Brazil

My home is in this huge new block of flats.

4

It has big windows, so I can see what goes on in the crowded street!

Helping at home

I help to clean the dishes!

dirty plate

6

Out and about

There is a forest near where I live!
We hike and cycle along the trails.

Fun

We hear music in the streets.

I love samba music!

We get snacks to eat on the go.

crisp little fish bites

My apartment is on the outskirts of town.

The best place for shopping is near us!

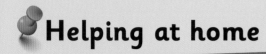

Helping at home

At lunchtime I set the table, and later I help clear up.

I love all sports – but a kickabout with my friends is the best of all!

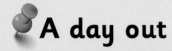

A day out

For a treat, we go to the animal park.

14

On the way home, we get
skewers of meat
as a snack.

16

There are crowds of other children to play with!

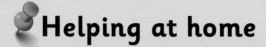

Helping at home

I don't mind tidying up! I help to keep my bedroom clean and smart.

18

Food

I love eating clear chicken soup with greens.

19

We like floating in a pedal boat on the lake!

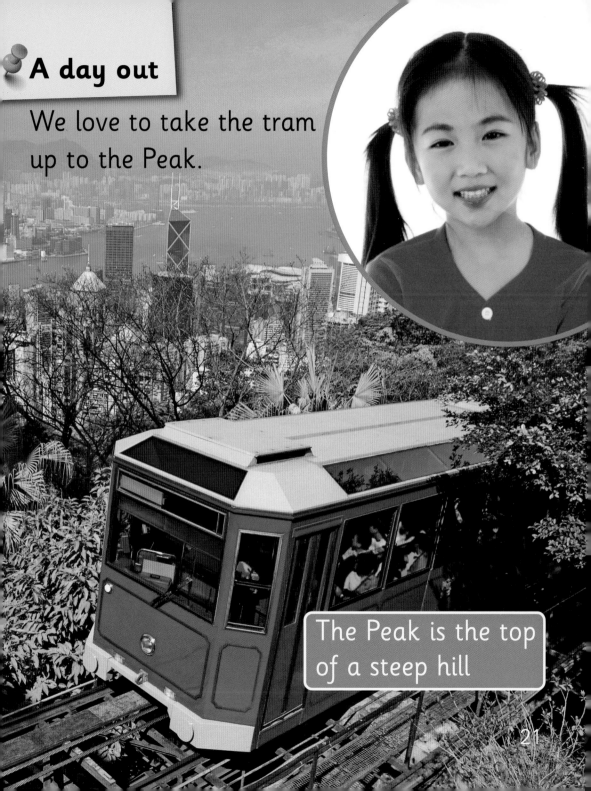

A day out

We love to take the tram up to the Peak.

The Peak is the top of a steep hill

21

Different and the same

homes

food

22

helping

fun

23

🐾 Review: After reading 🐾

Use your assessment from hearing the children read to choose any GPCs, words or tricky words that need additional practice.

Read 1: Decoding

- Challenge the children to find words in the book with "-s", "-ing" and "-ed" endings and to read them aloud:
  - –s (e.g. page 4 *flats*, page 5 *windows*, page 7 *trails*, page 8 *streets*, page 10 *outskirts*)
  - –ing (pages 6, 12, 18, 23 *helping*, page 11 *shopping*, page 20 *floating*)
  - –ed: (page 5 *crowded*)
- Ask the children to find words that contain the /oa/ phoneme (*home, go, windows*) and the /oo/ phoneme (*music, new, soup*) and discuss their different spellings.

Read 2: Prosody

- Take turns to read a page of text. Use a narrator's more formal tone for the chapter titles, subheadings and labels; use a more enthusiastic, expressive voice for each child in the book.
- Ask the children to locate a section using the contents list and headings, then read that section aloud. For example, say: Can you find and read the section about Ana?; Can you find and read the section about Eric?

Read 3: Comprehension

- For every question ask the children how they know the answer. Ask the children:
  - What is the same or different about the buildings? (e.g. *two are in blocks, the third isn't*)
  - What is the same or different about the food? (e.g. *all are cooked; one is a soup; one is on skewers*)
  - What is the same or different about how the children help? (e. g. *Ana and Eric help in the kitchen, but Eric has a dishwasher*)
  - What is the same or different about how they have fun? (e.g. *all go outdoors but only Ana says she likes music*)
- Ask the children to talk about their own home: where they live, how they help at home, their food and what they do for a fun day out.